Sparkle
and friends

UMⴲJA

a trademark of Unity Ink Press LLC

I0106227

Copyright © 2024 by Unity Ink Press LLC, Nevada

All Rights Reserved:

All rights are reserved by Unity Ink Press LLC. No part of this book may be reproduced by any means (mechanical or electronic) without written permission from Unity Ink Press LLC ("the Publisher"), except portions for the purpose of review or to share colored artwork on social media platforms. The content within this coloring book, including illustrations and accompanying text, is protected by copyright law. Reproduction, distribution, or any form of unauthorized use is prohibited.

ISBN: 979-8-9889846-3-4

This book belongs to:

Fun Coloring Tips:

For the best coloring experience, we recommend using colored pencils and/or alcohol-based markers. To ensure your artwork remains pristine, place a protective sheet of paper beneath the page you're working on to prevent any potential bleed-through.

Show Off Your Masterpiece with your Parent's Permission:

We're super excited to see your art and we'd love to see your unique creations come to life! Share your finished artwork on social media using #SparkleandFriends and tag @UmojaInkPress

More Fun Awaits:

Ask your parents for even more coloring pages! Visit UmojaInkPress.com. Download them, color away, and don't forget to share your cool creations with everyone!

Happy coloring, friend! Can't wait to see what you create!

Aaliyah

I am a leader and so are you.

Adalyn

I am a visionary and so are you.

Alicia

I am noble and so are you.

Amaya

I am charming and so are you.

Ashley

I am vibrant and so are you.

Ayesha

I am joyful and so are you.

Camila

I am gracious and so are you.

Ebony

I am dynamic and so are you.

Fatima

I am sincere and so are you.

Imani

I am virtuous and so are you.

Isabella

I am creative and so are you.

Jasmine

I am courageous and so are you.

Layla

I am inspirational and so are you.

Leilani

I am brave and so are you.

Makayla

I am radiant and so are you.

Maya

I am sophisticated and so are you.

Mei

I am confident and so are you.

Mira

I am unique and so are you.

Naomi

I am determined and so are you.

Nevaeh

I am powerful and so are you.

Olivia

I am wise and so are you.

Priya

I am friendly and so are you.

Sakura

I am enthusiastic and so are you.

Sparkle

I am adventurous and so are you.

Sydney

I am intelligent and so are you.

Zuri

I am brilliant and so are you.

www.ingramcontent.com/pod-product-compliance
Lightning Source LLC
Chambersburg PA
CBHW042342030426
42335CB00030B/3434